The Lizard Silence

Scottish Contemporary Poets Series

(for further details of this series please contact the publishers)

Gerry Cambridge, *The Shell House;* 1 898218 34 X
Jenni Daiches, *Mediterranean;* 1 898218 35 8
Valerie Gillies, *The Ringing Rock;* 1 898218 36 6
Kenneth Steven, *The Missing Days;* 1 898218 37 4
Brian Johnstone, *The Lizard Silence;* 1 898218 54 4
Siùsaidh NicNèill, *All My Braided Colours;* 1 898218 55 2
Ken Morrice, *Talking of Michelangelo;* 1 898218 56 0
Tom Bryan, *North East Passage;* 1 898218 57 9
Maureen Sangster, *Out of the Urn;* 1 898218 65 X
Anne MacLeod, *Standing by Thistles;* 1 898218 66 8
Walter Perrie, *From Milady's Wood;* 1 898218 67 6
William Hershaw, *The Cowdenbeath Man;* 1 898218 68 4

The Lizard Silence

Brian Johnstone

SCOTTISH CONTEMPORARY POETS SERIES

SCOTTISH CULTURAL PRESS

First published 1996
by Scottish Cultural Press
PO Box 106, Aberdeen AB11 7ZE
Tel: 01224 583777
Fax: 01224 575337

British Library Cataloguing in Publication Data
A catalogue for this book is available from the British Library

ISBN: 1 898218 54 4

The publisher acknowledges subsidy from the Scottish Arts Council
towards the publication of this volume

Printed and bound by
BPC-AUP Aberdeen Ltd.

Contents

I

In Remembrance   3
Shetland Times   4
Peat Diggings   4
Dead Crows   5
Gralloched Stag   6
Startled Doe   7
The Path o Licht   8
Mirk   8
Nicht Ploys   9
Westruther Muir   9
Crows on St Andrew's Day   10
Corpse   10
Composition   11
Meltwater   11
November   12
Gulls from Afar   13
Incident with Gull   14
Late Spring   15
Toad Calls   16

II

Concentration   19
Competition   20
Rite of Passage   21
Outward Bound   22
The Old Kettle   23
Moving On   24
Changing Shores   25
Some Potential   26
Improvement   27
Your Clicking Heart   28
The Upstairs Tenant   29
Le Coup d'Oeil   30
The Changing Patterns   31
Bill's Eye   32

Fred's Eye   33
On the Buchan Coast   34
Were the Day Clear   34
Groundwork   35
Journals Found   36
Skating on Happy Valley Pond   37
A String of Beads   38
The Mirror's Look   39
Raking Over Ashes   40

III

Which Sea   43
For Your Information   44
Deep Mani   45
The Church of Aghios Strategos   46
Water from the Well   47
On the South Coast of Crete   48
True to Form   49
Translation   50
For Good   51
The Deserted House   52
Landfall   53

Notes on the poems   54

Acknowledgements

Several of these poems have appeared in the following publications, to whose editors thanks are due: *Poetry Wales, Northwords, Spectrum, Understanding, Epoch, Inscape, Accents of Fife, Squibs, Northern Exposure, The Scottish Child, The Scots Magazine* and *The Scotsman.*
Illustration by Jean Eddy Johnstone.

Brian Johnstone was born in Edinburgh in 1950 but has lived in Fife since 1969. Although published while a student, he has only returned seriously to poetry in the last ten years.

In 1991 he co-founded *Shore Poets* in Edinburgh and in 1994 was co-editor of their first anthology *The Golden Goose Hour* (Taranis Books), a winner of the *Deric Bolton Poetry Trust* Publisher's Award. He has also been instrumental in founding the Poets on the Pier series of readings for the Pittenweem Arts Fesitval.

One of the artists and writers who created the exhibition *Landfall* for the 1993 St Andrews Festival, he has more recently been working with a multi-national group of poets and print makers whose limited edition folio has been purchased by the National Library of Scotland. Also active as a photographer, Brian Johnstone's solo exhibition, *The Shape of Time,* was shown in both St Andrews and Oxford during 1990.

His verse has been published widely in magazines, periodicals and anthologies and he has given readings in many parts of the country as well as on BBC Radio Scotland. *The Lizard Silence* is his first collection and features work from the last eight years.

commendably tight and meticulous like mosaics,
Stewart Conn

sensitive and master-crafty,
Tom Pow

strong and finished, with fine simplicity of language,
Gordon Meade

For Jean

I

In Remembrance

through the woods we take of them
the fruit of the thorn, the bramble

on the long path past the planting
beech and cherry, hazel and may

the light making pools innocent of effect
a greater green, the shape of a leaf

their eyes winking in the hedgerows
black as a cow's look, a crow's stare

touching the silky flesh to pull and pluck
we find we have no need, so ripe

a sweet rain falls into our palms
tongues grow purple of its taste

our wrists draw red in lines and dots
for this is my blood, its cost

Shetland Times

Why do I crave this land?
Its old bones picked so bare
by the ravening wind.

Why does this land so hold
my gaze? The hills and isles
prostrate before the storm.

Stand up! Get off your knees!
Why knuckle down to this
mere slide, the earth's slipstream?

Whale backed, beetle browed!
Living off the fat of the land
was never the way of it.

Peat Diggings

All is laid bare beyond the road
cut hard to turn and slope of land.

Peeled back and flayed of skin, the moor
shows lie of vertebrae and bone.

Here peat stacks clot the edge of wounds,
dry scabrous in the sun and wind.

The surgeon's hands stitch deep and well,
to quicken winter's cure, sew fire.

Dead Crows

In a landscape
of perfect circles
(sheep fanks on the moor's edge)
they beat as six black flags,
dead crows pinioned
on a wire.

Scaly jaws
clack open and leer
into the mist. Some wind
flaps their flesh and ruffles
their bones; so turn
in resurrection.

Cast down
to the earth, their eyes,
in sightless unison, forget
the sky and curse
the barbed wire's cut.
Damp's tears drop.

Dead nettles
in their crepe droop heads.
This autumn falls in grey
and black. On the moor
drifts of feathers speak
of some end.

Gralloched Stag

Taking our pace from silence,
our step from the winter air,
we left the track to lead us
where it would. It did.
Beyond the clearing's space,
a grim primeval beauty
met us stark and unprepared.
A gralloched stag strung up
and ripped from throat to pit.
Where knife and gravity
conspired, its stuff of life
heaped steaming in the chill.
We heard no shots, but here
man's steady hand had found
his rightful trove: a creature
in its running years and ways.
No broken twig, no footfall,
just the ebbing of its days.

Startled Doe

We breasted the hill
(sheep chomping at roots
away to the right) and,
coming down the long slope,
saw it stop and turn
and stop and take off
in a gust of limbs.

Freezing, just as *it* does,
we fix our gaze to the spot
and bind imaginations
to its loping grace.
It seeks the shadow
of a sapling, halts again
and casts a backward look.

Caught in its stare
we feel ourselves exposed,
two figures in the open,
open to mistrust. We watch it
thread from light to shade,
to safety in the distance,
trees and fallow ground.

The Path o Licht

Stracht fae the lang deep haas
o space, ae smaa
an fickle shaft o licht
eeks itsel oot
amang the trummlin shaws.
Whiles, through the saughs
an mang the birks an haws
the raydyance o
anither warld taks wing
an flits fae leaf
tae leaf till, happit in
the mirk, it dims an faas.

Mirk
(for Drew)

Twa sterns glistnin like bools
hing aboon the saughs
gracin the black leadit lift
wi sic a sperk o life
as wid kindle mair
faur ower mair
nor the dawn's gurly flame.

Nicht Ploys

The great neep heidit moon
stravaigs aboot the nicht
as muckle's a thoomb print
on a slide. An aa
the fine grammar
o the constellations,
pits tae shame
his gleg coorseness.

Smaa wunner the sterns
aye keep their distance
fae the likes o him.

Westruther Muir

Wi stoicism unboondit
the kye trauchle philosophic
mang the clerts an glaur
heedin nae mair the smirr
nor the sooch o wund.

Whiles, waefu an weary,
their orra cousins the tupps
hirple aboon the myre gress
hostin fae ower mony lang nichts.

Crows on St Andrew's Day

Wind buffeted, the crows sway
in their tree top world,
a caw-caw of conversation
as the old gossips
set the place to rights
putting the evil eye on anyone
who doesn't see beak to beak.
From chimneys below them
a reek of smoke
obscures their hooded shapes
bringing a soft focus fog
to dim their din
and make a forest
of the winter bare boughs
they dot with their black bulk.

Corpse

The cat has left some gems for me
amongst the grass.

Emeralds green a carnelian's gleam
between the blades.

I move. The jewelled backs of flies
take sudden wing.

A ruby bloods the ground beneath
with riven life.

She leaves for me the death she wrought
some hours ago.

Composition

stopping
        briefly
                on the track
the sharp smell of fox
invades
        my senses

on a step or more
and an almost
                perfect circle
of down and feathers

betrays his purpose
                by design

Meltwater

goose white
                the snow
takes river water
turns
        to granite grey
and goes

the ice   flaps on

shears
        like crystal
chitters
        like a flock
        of tiny birds
migrates
        downstream

November

this is the time
                of peeling
of damp
            lending its sheen of cold

a time
        when bareness
                        is not naked
but pitiful
            in its dress

watch
        as the yellow flags

                fly from the sycamore
wave
        in the hopeless wind

Gulls from Afar

Seurat's   brush   strokes

scarcely
     dry on their wing
               tips
a flock
    of
        termagant gulls
surges
    in a perfect arc
over
    the winter wheat

       black and white
       black and white

they
    shimmer
        like fish scales
in a
    blue wash
  of
       frosted air

Incident with Gull
(for Ade)

The noise demanded attention.

Mice, or rats, you thought
that dirled at the skirtings,
rattled up indignation,
and forced you downstairs.

You slept alone but
no better, no worse. The house
shook with a grim tap-tapping,
infesting your space.

A cupboard moved (you
saw it) but just a fraction
of an inch, though still too far
beyond its confines.

Behind, a blocked up
chimney held sooted feathers,
desperate eyes, a beak that
forced through plasterboard.

The gull survived another day.

Released, it hobbled
down the lawn, black and grimy.
A miner's blink, a grimace,
half forgotten light.

Feathers frayed with hours
shuffled back like cards into
the pack. Adults descended,
intent on their wrath.

A cuffing of wings,
a chattering of beaks as
it faced its loud accusers,
the fool upbraided.

You watched it scramble
to the wall-top, avoiding
chimneys, take the sky
for estuary mud.

The mice were another matter.

Late Spring

This is, I fancy, such as
Edward Thomas would have liked:

the strength of light
that casts the beech boughs
strong on a ground glass sky;

the new leaves bright
and banked and crowded,
green as the road goes by;

and every springtime sight,
each start of summer, there
in hopes and every hedge bird's cry.

Toad Calls

Of an evening
late at opening
the door, on site
I find him,
squat and blinking
back the night,
the unexpected guest,
toad caller
in the darkness
and the damp.

Crouching on the step,
all double chin
and gutta-percha back,
he takes fright
at owl call,
or the brightness
of the outside light,
and fights his way
outwith my gaze
to deep inviting black.

I think of him
ensconced in leaf mould,
right camouflaged,
jocose, a happy jack,
his vital panic
over for the night,
as, palpitating,
brown and warty,
sleep overtakes him,
pays him back.

II

Concentration

(for Osian)

the small boy
           turns
his curly head
this way
           and that

places
           one booted foot
then another
upon
           the highest
of the line of stones

looks about him
tenses
           and jumps

all the while
singing
           softly
to himself
a song
           suitable
to the sense
           of his task

Competition

Each boy finds his own.
A rock, a stone, a pebble.
Bankability no problem.
The beach has plenty to spare.

Turn over, touch, compare.
They have need of these.
Stumble to the shore.
A weight on their minds.

They take it in turns.
Underarm, a shoulder throw.
Heft them into the deep.
A means to an end.

The sea advances, extends.
Each places his bid.
The male of the species.
Making a splash.

Rite of Passage

Down sloping path and greasy steps
we gain the cutting. The forbidden,
we thrill at its touch, alone.

On to the line. A set of points
resists our strength. A can to kick
and ballast stones to rattle round inside.

'The wheels will suck you in,'
my mother said. A lie, no doubt. Still,
comes the train, headed for somewhere.

Backs against the wall, we wait
for our proof. Friends, daring each other.
Boys, being boys, being men.

A roar, that cloud of steam train smell,
it shudders by. My stare bobs
in the red light, sucked in alright.

Outward Bound

(for S.R.M.)

Out of the trees
you stopped. Above:
the ridge, a slope of scree
and there the weather waits,
a threat in line.

Look down, you see
that rock, that pine?
Gauge their size, agree
on what is relative to what
and what is not.

They climb, these children,
void of any fear, not
knowing why you're
stressing what you are
or why you care.

Perhaps the map will tell
a different tale,
will teach some notion
of the terrors of the place.
You hope in vain.

Later, when you turn,
they play a stupid game.
They hide from you in jest.
You recognise frustration,
ignorance of risk.

Your words have simply
vanished in the mist.
Imagination cannot
flesh the bones;
no touchstone's there.

A frown, you turn,
and look to where
the weather draws its hand
across the glass. You search
perhaps a quarter of an hour.

Found safe and laughing,
but the joke's turned sour.
A father's temper,
born of your distress;
you shame yourself.

Your son you scare;
as anger bites relief
and finds it bitter
to the taste, in silence,
trace your steps below.

The Old Kettle

veteran of a thousand picnics
they unwrap your patina
of woodsmoke and tar
cradled in last year's papers
against abuse
                    vaguely search
for stick and log apiece
upon that windswept beach
and kindle heat
                    placing
blackamoor, your grimy face
upon the continent of flame

Moving On

Last night in the old room we lie
just seeing the sky
through a gap in the shutters' plan.

Slowly our minds scan
the spending of time, the passage
of pleasure and age.

And through the house boxes all packed,
our memories stacked
between pans and china and chairs.

Significant cares
we take to a new bed, planting
there, time still wanting,

our future, like bulbs, layered deep
in the growing heap
that furnishes unfurnished space.

Hopes, regrets in place,
last night in the old room we lie
just seeing the sky.

Changing Shores
(for Ros)

I

Selling furniture and pans,
disposing of books,
you had already moved,
already gone away.

The little time left,
the slough of your home,
spurred the shedding
of a past you'd passed by.

Your eyes danced
bright and otherwhere:
that white house by the shore,
those boats at anchor.

Feet bare and brown,
oh lifestyles away,
you stepped remembered warmth
down lines of cold stone.

II

Come to say our farewells
we felt acquisitive:
rummaging encouraged,
impulses trying it on.

We took deckchairs
for the sun we hoped for,
music for the leavening,
books for the leisure time;

and you dashed with them
through a borrowed storm,
tropical rain stotting
on northern streets,

your shirt's silk
blotched with the patterns
of another continent,
arms heaped with goodbyes.

Some Potential

Viewing property defined in glowing terms
(desirable, affordable, needs little renovation)
we find the sad remainder of a life,
a husk still warm, a carapace unlaced,
the cold and damp intrusive on the memory displaced.

Examining the eaves, we poke and prod
for evidence, for bounty to our under-offer eye,
and, prying back the modesty of carpets,
we sniff and taste the air,
drawing dampness to the palate, recognise despair.

And everywhere the signs of life truncated,
two faded armchairs, ashtrays, flowerpots, a cooker
heir to stains, two unmatched gloves:
an old man living by endurance, by default,
caring for an acre as a ritual, as an afterthought.

Thinking this not ended, dragging to a close,
we prowl about the garden, try the doors of sheds,
seek out potential, find it
in six growing bulbs, emphatically restored:
a future lost without its mentor, quite ignored.

Improvement

We stripped the room so bare
nothing was left to the imagination.
An echo took up residence.
Ingrained, the ghosts of pictures
regarded us with dead eyes.

Drips of water traced their maps
as we scrubbed at time's deletions.
The ceiling grew great drops of sweat.
With plaster we stopped the cries
of cracks and hollows and holes.

Perched, we stabbed on the paint
while newspapers mosaiced the floor.
The ladders stalked about the room.
Gathering, advancing in storm clouds,
colour swept the walls away.

Sweating, we rubbed our aching arms
and hid in our new eyes.

Your Clicking Heart

The room is cold;
the stove, again run out of coal,
clicks broken panes
before a gusting wind.

You stare at pane
and half pane, vainly searching for
the one that clicks
against some dozen odds;

and think of trust
and confidence, prey to the wind.
The cracks behind
this clicking drive you mad;

one is the cause
(or one at any time, it's true)
but watch them each
in turn, no culprit's found.

You stare at pain;
it stares straight back at you. Alone
your clicking heart
desires the wind to die.

The Upstairs Tenant

Golden girl
the black angel touched you.
Stuck in that 'wonderful dream'
you took root.

Upstairs the boards
ached with your footsteps,
throbbed in their grain: no sleep,
no sleep.

A kind of winter
had seeped through your bars,
easing its fabric under the sill,
easing your will.

A perforation of space,
a spore driven agony that
troubled your friends not enough,
drove you to this.

Door sealed,
a mother's milk in cups,
you stepped back to view your work,
to take it further.

Golden girl,
your goose is cooked now,
done to a crisp. Spit in his face.
Go on.

for Sylvia Plath

Le Coup d'Oeil – un film
(for Adele)

Provence. A hilltop cafe-bar. Few patrons save
a pock marked man, a woman half his age, the cat.

A car draws up. Your husband, the painter, yourself.
You take a seat. The view unfolds below the rail.

'Trois express.' You wait. The seats are hard.
The painter ups an eyebrow, turns his mouth aside.

'Ne regardez pas, mais...c'est votre Durrell.'
The message registers. Your eyes flick left.

A man not old but rounded, smoothed with age,
shares his table, fields some conversation.

Your talk continues. A hero? Not in so many words.
'Peut-etre...tu le connais?' The head just shakes.

That negative damns an introduction. You sigh.
Each drinks some coffee. The afternoon wears on.

The cafe is an eyrie, its valley a hunting range.
Captured are yourselves, this writer, this woman.

A gambit. A sudden need to stretch, to see the view.
You slip out from your chair, move towards the rail.

Their discourse is beyond your ear. You cannot know,
you cannot steal a morsel. Durrell's eyes swing round.

A second slips between you. Eyes that met with Clea's
catch your look. *'Monsieur, permettez-moi...'* But no.

The writer turns. He makes to rise. You smile
but each thinks better and the moment's past.

What would have been? You know what would have been.
'Mais dites! Cet homme est peu ouvert.' No point.

The day, the time, the summer passed. Two months.
You hear, the writer Durrell obituaried and dead.

You think of words, of thoughts not quite exchanged.
He wrote once...'better leave the rest unsaid'.

The Changing Patterns

I lie here
listening to you sleep,
the changing patterns
of your breathing,
tiny sighs and moans
the evidence of life;
and worry that the crack
will open
swallow you again.

I turn over,
try to clear my mind,
your ghost comes dripping
from the sea.
I watch the water
lap against imaginings
and slip my hand,
cupped hopefully,
below your sleeping head.

Bill's Eye

a tiny
oh so
insignificant detail

caught Bill's eye
as homeward
car-bound

one
December
night of

thick and
deepening
fog

he saw
in that precise
discerning way

a synchronicity
of time
and place

that now
by courtesy
of print and book

hangs on the page
a photograph
he took

for William Carlos Williams

Fred's Eye

the flatiron building
huge
against the sky

the shining pavements
umbrellas
wet with rain

the city
halting in its tracks awhile
he stopped

and you were there
you saw it
kept it so

the line
of trunk and back
in balance in your eye

you caught him
as he bent
out from the kerb

a man
a wayside tree
a verse in black and white

this poem which
you sometime wrote
in light

for Alfred Stieglitz

On the Buchan Coast

That day in the Gamrie
bright as a mussel's sheen,
you picked a feather
from the pier-head, stole
lightness from the air.

Houses, spruce in rows,
put on all whites and blues,
shook out their curtains
and their smoke, days
a little numbered even so.

And walking by the shore
we skimmed those stones
swift as a gannet's eye,
those smooth and feathered ones
that wander briefly into hope.

Were the Day Clear

When he was not fishing
enforced idleness hung on his shoulders
like an old oilskin
and he would moor himself
hulk-like
to a public bench at the pier-head
(stones jewelled with fish scales;
air bright with reflections)
and gaze with seal eyes
to where he would place the horizon
were the day clear.

Groundwork
(for C.E.E.)

When you went there first
they mistook you for the gardener.

An old bunnet, scythe in hand
and the practiced sweep of the blade.

Bothying for the while,
your oil lamps flickered at night.

The study warmed to your thoughts,
a gasper never far from your mind.

Each Sunday you rang the bell,
marked the seasons, their passing.

Frayed like the gown and mortar,
your dungarees stayed on.

Ready to turn a hand, drive a nail,
your contrivances dotted the place:

Your *life* was never like that,
but a weeding out, a potting on.

They took you for the gardener
back then, supposing it was so.

Journals Found

In that cupboard familiar since childhood
two things stood out: notebooks in their red gloss,
a rote of rods and perches, reams and quires
indicative of age. Unfamiliar, they drew the eye.

No name, no title and the script not *quite* unknown
prompted a request. I should have recognised
that stately hand, remembered calmly spoken thoughts
and quiet eyes, a grandmother's age and depth.

Years turned, decades and childhoods gone, and here
a conversation with the past, a journey which you took
I never knew. I turn the pages, hear your voice
and see again your smile as soft as rain.

This time I mean to listen well. I take the books,
your journals of a world I need to travel too.

Skating on Happy Valley Pond
(for my mother)

On nights of chill but little frost
they would flood the tennis courts
allowing a film of ice to form.

A small band played. You danced,
a hand-made dress of tourquoise and black
swirling, like dreams, about you.

And came the greater chill,
the harder frost to freeze the pond,
a happy valley opened at your feet.

The chance support of water in a skin
snapped wings upon your heels, gave grace
its romance, space its sporting chance.

A flash of blades, the lifelines
turned across the ice, opposing,
crossing, merging at your will.

And later, when the fire was lit,
you sat between the knees of men and boys,
held briefly in the slow suspense of time.

A String of Beads

It begins with a taking apart.

The cord cut
in their dozens
they tumble into my palm.

Discard but one,
the cause of this,
chipped, outlandish, out of place.

The unforseen, the unprepared for.

Laid in lines,
for a time, play
their rythms like a game of draughts.

Fathomed at last,
sorted and heaped,
a fresh pattern presents itself.

Ease into it as it becomes apparent.

A new knot,
it begins again,
a long rethreading in time.

They clack back
positions reversed,
counted in like returning planes.

So it ends, with a new wearing.

The Mirror's Look

Times like these
he stares back at me
in the glass, my father
dead these twenty years
but growing in
the mirror's look,
my other face.

His beard my beard,
I shave his bristle
to the bowl;
I walk his walk,
run at his pace;
his nakedness shakes
my spreading frame.

And others too,
they see him there,
in photographs,
in passing glances;
in the subtle turnings
of the inner eye:
my passenger.

Accepting this,
I grasp the hand,
respect as truth
these echoes of the man;
take on the ghost
I fought against,
misunderstood.

Raking Over Ashes

Some afternoon, the winter light
low and slanting through the panes,
I stoop to lay another fire.

Raking the ashes, poker in hand,
metal strikes metal and, looking closer
I find it, bent beyond recognition.

An old screw nail, burnt from a hole,
unwitting time has led to here.
I turn it slowly in my hand.

Memories cast up and fall away
as easily as the rust idly
I flake off with the back of my thumb.

That nail, found where least sought;
my thoughts sink back into the ash;
I stoop to lay another fire.

III

Which Sea

The eye of the cowrie,
belly of the whelk;
each cast a different wave.

Which sea's ghost
rushes and hums
in their murmurous depths?

Shell-like to shell
the ear seeks out the mystery,
explores the space.

The mind, for its part,
threads cowrie to cowrie sound
and takes

of the whelk's great boomings:
oceans, all past,
aeons of clamour, drowned.

For your Information
(for Jan)

οροϛ ειμι τηϛ αγοραϛ
Inscription on boundary stone of
the Greek Agora, Athens – 500 BC

the stone says
I am the boundary
of the agora
I am the end
and the beginning
the stone says
here are welcome
free men
here I embrace you
make your choices
make your decisions
take time
the stone says
two thousand years
and more
I will still be here
I have my work
cut out

Deep Mani

Towering over towers
that haunt with grace
this land stripped to the bone,
cloud catching Kakovouni
steals the sun.

Marching upwards,
dykes grey vein the slopes
while stones prepare attacks
on still unconquered space.

Here the lizard silence
flicks his tail in mute contempt
and darts between the rocks
to lie, unseen in ambush,
awaiting time
propitious for revenge.

The Church of Aghios Strategos

Expecting some refusal of locks,
with slight anticipation
I try the door. It gives. Surprised
I slide into the oily gloom
and wait. My eyes take care,
rehearse the scales of light
and dark. In time, a thousand years
stand gaping in the gap
between these walls and me.
As quiet as the grave, they say,
but this is something more:
a silence self-absorbed, exhaled
through frescoed lips and nostrils
flared in paint. The walls recede,
their peopled surface pitted
but unbowed. These men
remember nothing. Their thoughts
are tidy plaster heaps in cracks
dry as the bones in boxes
by the door. They frown.
I stand an age or more
watching the past in painted robes
indifferent, watching me.

Water from the Well
(for Father John)

On the island is a mountain
ridged with crenellations,
and Chorio, the abandonded place,
walls stood about
in solitude, like the dead.

Two doors are left. We find them,
high on the hill path
stepped in the rock,
and a courtyard,
cypress shaded, pebbled in peace.

The church, locked and fast,
guards its treasures:
Christouyenna, Epitaphios, Paskha;
the ritual of time,
the passage to healing and grace.

We turn. Cord slips from the latch:
the other, a white room
bare and pure as thought,
cradles the well,
sweetest water on the island, so they say.

A can on a rope; I let it fall,
a minute in the void
till it rises brim full of echoes,
the knowledge
of its passage in the stone.

'Wisdom, *Sophia*,' the priest had intoned,
late at the year's end.
We take the water and drink,
chill from the rock,
cool and clear, like understanding.

On the South Coast of Crete

A low lap-lapping as a cat at milk
the waves caress the shore.
Each stone is rounded
imperceptibly more
by this languid pulse, this slow persuasion,

while at anchor the colour blue resolves
itself into a boat.
The hillside, tricked out
with flocks of sheep and goats,
defines the quiet with each clonking bell.

Sounds mingle in the listless breath of noon.
Olive stones round my plate
measure out the moods
I can't articulate.
A dozen birds, smaller than any fist,

flock to the tree that each had chosen first.
Their suddeness imparts
a strange unity
of purpose to their art.
The tree shakes, less in anger than in mirth.

True to Form

It was the dog that led us there,
emerging from the woods, Pan to our credulity.
Down shadowed paths all crisp with olive leaves
and the bloodstain gout of fallen fruit on stones,
our boots believed and followed in his wake.
A cry from houses – nothing, just a cock,
and somewhere in the hillside donkeys snort.
The sun is far off, flickering through the trees,
as, pad-pad, on he goes,
his black and white a shadow in itself.

The track leads down and up and down,
a slope as gradual as that,
until through thinning trees
the light defines some space.
A valley that this dog has conjured up
from nowhere, sloping green and scrub-clad,
cliffed and rocked, remote.

We're lost, we know, in contemplation
of the place, a minute or an hour,
but lose our guide to find him true to form
and sphinx-like at the purpose of his walk.

Behind us, in the curtain of the woods,
in stone a curdled, milky grey,
two covered wells seem pyramids to our eyes.
The one, a bolted fastness,
minds its treasure guardedly
while black space and a broken open door
have their protector in this canine Pan.
He lies, two forepaws side by side,
in mute heraldic pose, his black and white
all black beneath the cooling shade.
And wise as working dogs become
he shows us to the well and to the wealth within.

Translation

A single lightbulb
hangs by the door.
An empty terrace,
a view to the sea.
Two towels flap
slightly in the breeze.
The railings rust.
The house of Ritsos
lies by the walls.

A bunch of flowers
fades in the light.
A wooden cross,
a name, a forename,
front a mound of earth.
The sun shines.
Stones show respect.
The grave of Ritsos
lies by the shore.

An ancient photo
in a split new frame.
A shelf of books
in the tourist shops.
Relatives keen to talk.
The road he took away
snakes round the rock.
The life of Ritsos
lies safely done.

for Yannis Ritsos

For Good

In the Great Western Road
we drink our *kafedakia*
and discuss Kalamata olives.

The smiling man slaps his stomach
and shows us his village
on a faded map. Aghios Andreas,
St Andrews, lost in the north.
He thinks of his parents' house
and of the lamb and potatoes
he will eat on Sunday.

Meanwhile, south of the Green Line,
they talk and talk. Cyprus
is red in blood and poppies
but wears its wounds well.
Still, our host can never see
his birthplace again.

On the telephone an hour
his son has a Glasgow accent.
They have quit the eastern road
for good, or something of the sort.

The Deserted House

At first it was the door that wondered,
the last touch still on the latch.
Atrophied by rust, the hinges kept their peace.

In the day the shutters wondered,
their rituals unperformed.
Wind picked at the slats, vines tightened their grip.

Within the floorboards wondered.
No tread, no footfall,
no single creak to disturb their train of thought.

In the dim light the bed wondered,
brass greying with age,
the pillows bereft, without the slightest impression.

The mirror too, it wondered,
seeing no face to know.
Clouds and specks peopled its reflections with doubt.

Alone with their thoughts, all wondered
as dust motes danced.
The last head, it had turned, had not returned.

And in time the stones wondered,
outside in the bitter street;
and the days passed and the footsteps never came.

Landfall

This is the story of the waves.

A deep roar, a swell to break a back,
a breast to heave a year upon.

This is the story of the tide.

Each step taken, two steps back;
knowledge and certainty, some little hope.

This is the story of the helm.

A fast friend, the arc of the sky;
companion of the empty hours.

This is the story of the reef.

Bared teeth to greet a man and say:
time to stand off, to reflect awhile.

This is the story of the strand.

A woman's welcome, golden, afire,
soft and fine upon the eye.

This is the story of the keel.

Seeking for purchase, a holding shot;
a fist that falls in absence of doubt.

This is the story of the step.

Take it if you wish no favour;
it is of no import, no consequence at all.

This is the story of the land.

Wounded to the touch of a man,
it cannot be freed, it cannot get away.

Notes on the Poems

I

p. 5, Dead Crows
Sheep fanks are walled circular enclosures for the containing of sheep, common on Scottish moors.

p. 6, Gralloched Stag
The process of gralloching involves the gutting of a deer, usually performed by the hunter immediately on killing the animal.

p. 8, The Path o Licht
trumlin – trembling
shaws – a grove of trees
saughs – willows
birks – birches
haws – hawthorns
happit – wrapped
mirk – darkness
faas – falls

p. 8, Mirk
mirk – darkness
sterns – stars
bools – marbles
saughs – willows
lift – sky
gurly – flattering

p. 9, Nicht Ploys
neep – turnip
stravaigs – wanders
muckle – large
gleg – eager
sterns – stars

p. 9, Westruther Muir
kye – cattle
trauchle – drudge
clerts – muck
glaur – mud
smirr – drizzle
sooch – sucking
waefu – woeful
orra – occasional
tups – rams
hirple – stumble
aboon – above
hostin – coughing

p. 13, Gulls from Afar
Seurat was the leading painter of the Impressionist school known as *Pointillist* from the use of innumerable tiny dots of pigment to build up the picture overall.

II

p. 29, The Upstairs Tennant
On the evening before she took her life Sylvia Plath called on her downstairs neighbour. Opening his door an hour or so later, he found her still standing where he had left her. She said that she had been having a wonderful dream and did not want it to end. One of her last actions was to leave two cups of milk by her sleeping children's beds.

p. 30, *Le Coup d'Oeil*
This poem is based on a true story related to me by a friend.
coup d'oeil – glance
peu ouvert – literally, not very open

p. 33, *Fred's Eye*
Based principally on *Spring Showers, New York* by Stieglitz – a photographer roughly contemporaneous with Carlos Williams and who shares his economy of image.

p. 34, *On the Buchan Coast*
The Gamrie – the Doric name for Gardenstown, a fishing village on the north coast of Buchan.

p. 35, *Groundwork*
This poem is about my father-in-law, the Rev Crichton Eddy, minister in the Lammeruir Hills from 1948–82.

p. 37, *Skating on Happy Valley Pond*
Craiglockhart Pond in Edinburgh was formerly known as Happy Valley Pond. It was popular for ice dancing, a favourite pastime of my mother's, in the period leading up to the start of the Second World War. With thanks to Robin Williamson for the title, a line from his song *Koeeoaddi There.*

III

p. 44, *For Your Information*
The inscription on the boundary stone of the Agora is literally translated as 'I am the boundary of the Agora'. The Agora was not just a market but a meeting place for the free citizens of Athens, where debates took place and votes were cast.

p. 45, *Deep Mani*
The Mani, the most southerly peninsula of the Peloponnese, is a rocky and remote area which was never subdued by the Turks during their occupation of Greece and where the War of Independence began. It was also an area rife with internecine feuds. Families defended their honour and territory by building towers from which stones were frequently thrown as weapons of war. Kakovouni is the mountain running down the spine of the peninsula.

p. 46, *The Church of Aghios Strategos*
An eleventh-century Byzantine church near Anno Boulari also in The Mani. Since the tourist expansion in Greece it is usual to find churches locked. It is a custom of the Greek Orthodox Church to dig up the remains of buried corpses and store the bones in ossuaries.

p. 47, *Water from the Well*
Set on the small island of Halki, in the Dodecanese.
Christouyenna – Christmas
Epitaphios – the Easter service of Christ's burial
Paskha – the Easter service of Christ's resurrection
Sophia – the Greek for wisdom

p. 48, *On the South Coast of Crete*
Written about the tiny village of Loutro in Sfakia, the remote and inacessible part of south-west Crete.

p. 49, *True to Form*
This took place on the Ionian island of Paxos. As Peter Levi says in *The Hill of Kronos*, it is common for travellers in Greece to feel the presence of the ancient deities.

p. 50, *Translation*
Yannis Ritsos, one of the leading Greek poets of the twentieth century, was a lifelong communist and was villified for his opinions by a large section of the Greek population. He was born and is buried in Monemvassia, an ancient settlement in the Peloponnese. The simple grave marker refered to in the poem has now been replaced with a marble monument.

p. 51, *For Good*
This is set in a Greek delicatessen in Glasgow, now alas closed.
kafedakia – small cups of Greek coffee
Kalamata olives – reputedly the best olives in Greece
Aghios Andreas (translates as St Andrews) – on the Karpas peninsula of Cyprus, in the area invaded by the Turkish army in 1974 and to which all Greeks are prevented from returning
the Green Line – the UN patrolled line between the Turkish occupied north and the free southern part of the country

p. 52, *The Deserted House*
Travelling in Greece one frequently comes across houses deserted for many reasons, the two principal ones being economic necessity and political persecution.